PRAYER AND POWER

IN THE

CAPITAL

compiled *by Pauline Innis*

Prayer and Power in the Capital
compiled by Pauline Innis

copyright 1982

printed in the USA

The Devon Publishing Company, Incorporated
        Washington D.C.

Distributed by Caroline House
Aurora, Illinois

ISBN 0-941402-02-9

CONTENTS

LIST OF ILLUSTRATIONS

The Old Treasury was built in 1800 on the site of the present building. It was burnt in 1814 and rebuilt in 1817. In 1833 it was torn down to make way for the building that stands today. The Old Treasury was used by many denominations for their church service. Presbyterians worshipped here in the early years and also in the Georgetown Treasury building.

The Baptists who had received much harassment in Virginia, also held services here. The July 1st issue of the Museum Newspaper in 1801, carried the notice that "Mr. Richards, of the Baptist Church of Baltimore, will preach in the Treasury Office next Sunday."

TO
ALL THOSE WHO,
IN SPITE OF BUSY LIVES, HIGH OFFICE
AND THE PRESSURES OF POWER,
SPARED TIME TO SHARE WITH US THE SOURCE OF
THEIR INSPIRATION.
AND TO MY COUSIN
THE RIGHT REVEREND LAWRENCE E. LUSCOMBE
50th BISHOP OF BRECHIN, SCOTLAND,
IN MEMORY OF DAYS GONE BY.

**More things are wrought by prayer,
than most men dream of.**

Tennyson.

his book states simply the existing relationships
between prayer and those in power in Washington
D.C. and gives the prayers which have sustained our
leaders, hoping others will be inspired by them. It
does not attempt to decry, defend or extol the moral
standards or religious beliefs of those in power, but it does
analyse some of the effects of the power of prayer when used
by those in powerful places.

Persons in positions of power are subject to enormous
pressures and stress. They have the pressures of office as well
as the pressures of everyday life. As much of their time is spent
in the full glare of publicity, they have to be on guard lest they
say or do something which can be wrongly construed. Also,
persons in power have now become the target of assassins
and kidnappers in all parts of the world, so they need to pray
and be prayed for.

For some, prayer and meditation have become their
sustaining power and their means of relaxation and
refreshment. These were asked to share their favorite prayer or
meditation with us. As you see from these pages, many replied,
not only with a prayer, but with some personal thoughts and
anecdotes which were both heartwarming and inspiring. An
unexpected depth of understanding, kindness and compassion
shone through these letters. I hope you will get the same feeling
of renewed enthusiasm from the prayers as I did.

Some people said that their prayers were too personal to
share, others did not reply. There are others who were not
available at the time prayers were being collected and we hope
these will share their prayers in another edition. Some prayers
were taken from the Congressional Record. These are so
marked.

This unusual view shows the White House on the banks of Tiber Creek, also known as Goose Greek. This spur of the Potomac River was made the western terminus of a canal which extended east through the city of the Capitol, thence south in two branches to rejoin the river. It was filled in about 1870. The original owner of the land on which the White House stands was Davie Burns, a Scotchman, who lived in a cottage on the river bank. Like other large land owners he became wealthy with the increased value of his property.

The government encountered much difficulty in settling with the land owners, but an agreement was finally brought about whereby the land taken for public buildings was to be paid for at £25 per acre, while the part used for streets was to be relinquished without cost. The remainder was to be disposed of by public sale of lots, the proceeds going half to the owners and half to be spent in the erection of government buildings.

The executive affairs of the President were conducted in the White House until 1903, when a new office building was erected a short distance away on the White House grounds.

Tiber Creek
Also Known As Goose Creek

From: Bank of New York Calendar 1943

PRAYERS
OF THE PRESIDENTS OF
THE UNITED STATES OF AMERICA

WHITE HOUSE AND TIBER CREEK, 1840

PRESERVE ME O GOD FOR IN THEE DO I PUT MY TRUST

PSALM 16:1

Window of The Meditation Chapel
United States Senate

lmighty God, we make our earnest prayer that Thou will keep the United States in Thy Holy Protection, that Thou wilt incline the hearts of the citizens to cultivate a spirit of subordination and obedience to the government and entertain a brotherly affection and love for one another and for their fellow citizens of the United States at large, and finally, that Thou wilt most graciously be pleased to dispose us all to do justice, to love mercy, and to demean ourselves with that charity, humility and specific temper of mind which were the characteristics of the Divine Author of our blessed religion and without a humble imitation of example in these things we can never hope to be a happy nation.

Grant our supplications, we beseech Thee through Jesus Christ our Lord. Amen

Composed by *George Washington* in June 1783 while he was still Commander in Chief of the Continental Army.

John Adams

✡ ✡ ✡ ✡ ✡ ✡ ✡ ✡

I pray Heaven to Bestow
The best of Blessings on
THIS HOUSE
And all that shall here after
Inhabit it. May none but Honest
And Wise men ever rule under This Roof.

This prayer was written by *John Adams* and sent to his wife Abigail. President Adams wrote it on his second night in the White House in 1800. This prayer is engraved in the marble above the fireplace in the State Dining Room.

Thomas Jefferson

lmighty God, Who has given us this good land for our heritage; we humbly beseech Thee that we may always prove ourselves a people mindful of Thy favor and glad to do Thy will. Bless our land with honorable industry, sound learning and pure manners.

Save us from violence, discord and confusion; from pride and arrogance, and from every evil way.

Defend our liberties and fashion into one united people the multitude brought hither out of many kindreds and tongues.

Endow with the spirit of wisdom those to whom in Thy Name we entrust the authority of government, that there may be justice and peace at home and that through obedience to the law, we may show forth Thy praise among the nations of the earth.

In time of prosperity, fill our hearts with thankfulness and, in the day of trouble, suffer not our trust in Thee to fail; all of which we ask through Jesus Christ our Lord, Amen.

Written by *Thomas Jefferson*, President of the United States. Dec. 6 1801.

Grover Cleveland

✩✩✩✩✩✩✩

 nto God's gracious care we commit thee. The Lord bless and keep thee. The Lord make His face to shine upon thee and be gracious unto thee and give thee peace now, and forever more. Amen.

When *Grover Cleveland* married his young ward, Frances Folsom, his brother, the Reverend Will Cleveland gave this blessing. It was especially requested by President Cleveland.

Rutherford B. Hayes

O Lord our Heavenly Father, who has safely brought us to the beginning of this day; Defend us in the same with Thy Almighty power. Grant that we may not fall into any kind of danger and keep us from evil. May all our doings be ordered by Thy governance so that all we do may be righteous in Thy sight. Amen.   author unknown.

President and *Mrs. Hayes* said this prayer with their family every morning. Mrs. Hayes brought morning prayer to the White House. On Sunday evenings cabinet members and congressmen joined in the Sunday evening hymn singing with President and Mrs. Hayes.

Benjamin Harrison

✿ ✿ ✿ ✿ ✿ ✿ ✿ ✿

ark, the herald angels sing,
Glory to the newborn King.
Peace on earth and mercy mild
God and sinners reconciled.
Joyful all ye nations rise
join the triumph of the skies
    With the angelic host proclaim
Christ is born in Bethlehem
    Hark the herald angels sing
Glory to the newborn King.
           C. Wesley.

On Christmas Eve 1889, *Benjamin Harrison* brought the first Christmas tree into the White House. It was placed in the Oval room on the second floor and all the members of his family and some staff members helped decorate it.

On Christmas day President and Mrs. Harrison were joined by many friends and their families who joined in the singing of Carols around the tree. Hark The Herald Angels Sing, was a great favorite.

et us have faith
That right makes might,
That a single star
Illumines night.
That the weakest link
will hold the chain.

Written by *Abraham Lincoln* who once said, "I have been driven many times to my knees by the overwhelming conviction that I have nowhere else to go. My own wisdom and that of all about me seem insufficient for that day."

President Lincoln's words were not appreciated during his lifetime. The famous Gettysburg address was scarcely noticed, yet it stands as one of the most famous speeches of all time and a perfect example of simple eloquence. The short prayer given above was written at the outbreak of the Civil War.

Woodrow Wilson

✩✩✩✩✩✩✩✩

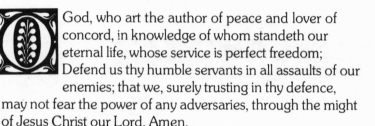

O God, who art the author of peace and lover of concord, in knowledge of whom standeth our eternal life, whose service is perfect freedom; Defend us thy humble servants in all assaults of our enemies; that we, surely trusting in thy defence, may not fear the power of any adversaries, through the might of Jesus Christ our Lord, Amen.

Author Unknown.

This prayer was often used by President Wilson who will be remembered for all his efforts on behalf of the League of Nations.

Franklin D. Roosevelt

, God whose power is limitless, make us believe that the only limit to our realisation of tomorrow is our doubt of today. Help us to move forward with a strong and active faith so that we can realise the potential of our nation and of ourselves. Amen.

Written by *Franklin Delano Roosevelt,* a great man who was an inspiration to those fighting proverty or sickness of body or soul.

Harry S. Truman

✫ ✫ ✫ ✫ ✫ ✫ ✫ ✫

ur Father, which art in Heaven,
Hallowed be Thy Name,
Thy Kingdom come,
Thy Will be done on earth
As it is in Heaven.
Give us this day our daily bread,
And forgive us our trespasses
As we forgive those
Who trespass against us.
And lead us not into temptation
But deliver us from evil.

Amen.

Harry S. Truman said the Lord's Prayer regularly,
however, he had a short prayer he wrote himself which seems
to express the practical side of his personality.

Lord, get me moving
And keep me going,
So long as you have work
For me to do. Amen.

Dwight D. Eisenhower

lmighty God, as we stand here at this moment my future associates in the executive branch of government join me in beseeching that Thou will make full and complete our dedication to the service of the people in the throng and their fellow citizens everywhere.

Give us we pray, the power to discern clearly right from wrong, and allow all our words and actions to be governed thereby, and, by the laws of this land.

Especially we pray that our concern shall be for all the people regardless of station, race or calling.

May cooperation be permitted and be the mutual aim of those, who, under the concepts of our Constitution, hold to differing political faiths; so that all may work for the good of our beloved country and Thy glory. Amen.

Written by *President Eisenhower* for his first inauguration, January 20th 1953.

John F. Kennedy

✿ ✿ ✿ ✿ ✿ ✿ ✿

Ask not what your country can do for you,
Ask what you can do for your country.
Ask not what God will do for you,
But rather what God wants you to do for Him.

John Fitzgerald Kennedy

Just a few months before his death President Kennedy spoke to the Congressional Prayer Breakfast concluding with these words.

"This morning we pray together, this evening apart, but each morning and each evening, let us remember the advice of my fellow Bostonian, the Reverend Phillips Brooks, 'Do not pray for easy lives, pray to be stronger men. Do not pray for tasks equal to your powers, pray for powers equal to your tasks."

During the short years of his Presidency, John F. Kennedy had a tremendous following among young people who saw this President and his young family as leaders of a modern Camelot.

Lyndon B. Johnson

 e come before Thee with grateful hearts, thankful for the days that have been ours and for the works we have been permitted to do together. In these hours now, our thoughts are not of ourselves but of our country.

Thou has blessed America greatly; may we, in the conduct of her affairs, be always worthy in Thy sight—and in the sight of our fellow man.

Deliver us from the follies of power and pride. Show us the uses of our strengths that will make life better on this earth for all Thy children. In season and out, help us to hold to the purposes Thou has taught us, feeding the hungry, healing the sick, caring for the needy, trusting our young, training them in the way that they should go.

Lift our visions, Father, renew our faith in Thee and in ourselves. Stir our spirits and disturb our consciences that we may seek not rest from our labors but right for our neighbors. Blind our eyes to the colors of men's skins, close our hearts against hate and violence, and will our souls with a love of justice and compassion.

May we, as a nation, deserve no enemies and be worthy of all our friends, striving without ceasing for a day when mankind shall not know war anymore.

Watch over this city and keep it from strife and sorrow.
Guard this Republic and guide us in its service.
These things we ask in Thy name. Amen.

This is the text of a prayer written by *President Johnson* and read at the National City Christian Church in Washington D.C.

Prayer is a very personal thing, at least for me. Yet, to me, as many of my predecessors, it is a terribly important source of strength and confidence. I have discovered another aspect of the power of prayer. I have learned how important it is to have people pray for me. It is often said that the Presidency is the loneliest job in the world. Yes, and in a certain sense, I suppose it is. Yet, in all honesty, I cannot say I have suffered from loneliness in these past six months.

The reason, I am certain, has been that everywhere I go people call out, or say quietly to me, "we are praying for you."

My own prayer is for God's continued blessing and God's continued guidance for our country and all its people whose servants we in government strive to be.

Gerald Ford speaking to the National Prayer Breakfast 1975. President Ford had the difficult task of bringing stability to the Administration after Watergate.

☆☆☆☆☆☆☆☆☆

ehold, I stand at the door, and knock: If any man hear my voice, and open the door, I will come in to him, and will sup with him, and he with me.

This is the prayer of Jesus to the people in Revelations 3:20. It is the favorite of Jimmy Carter.

Speaking to the National Prayer Breakfast in 1978, President Carter said,

To me, God is real. To me, the relationship with God is a very personal thing. God is ever present in my life. He sustains me when I am weak, gives me guidance when I turn to Him, and provides for me, as a christian, through the life of Christ, a perfect example to emulate in my experiences with other human beings. My wife and I worship together every night. Often, during the day, I turn to God in a very personal way.

☆ ☆ ☆ ☆ ☆ ☆ ☆ ☆

This unknown author wrote of a dream and in this dream he was walking down a beach beside the Lord and, as they walked, above him in the sky was reflected each stage and experience of his life. And, reaching the end of the beach and of his life, he turned back down the beach and saw the two sets of footprints in the sand except that he looked again and saw that every once in a while there was only one set of footprints, and when there was only one set of footprints it was when the experience reflected in the sky was one of great despair, desolation, grief and trial in his life.

He turned to the Lord and said, "You said that if I would always walk with you, You would be beside me and take my hand. Why did you desert me? Why are you not there in times of trouble when I need You?"

The Lord said," My child I did not leave you. When you saw only one set of footprints, It was there that I carried you. . ."

I know that in the days to come and the years ahead there are going to be many times when there will be only one set of footprints in my life. If I did not believe that, I could not face the days ahead.

President Reagan speaking at the National Prayer Breakfast.   Congressional Record.

St. John's Church, Lafayette Square, The Church of the Presidents
as it appeared in 1816

The burning of Washington in 1814 interrupted plans to build
St. John's but, confident that the city would rise again from the ashes,
plans went ahead and it was completed and consecrated in 1816. St.
John's was designed by Latrobe who refused any compensation for his
work. Latrobe also wrote the dedicatory hymn. The bell of St. John's
was cast in the foundry of Joseph Revere, son of the famous Paul. Its
proximity to the White House makes it very popular with the
Presidents.

Henry Foxall of Philadelphia and his partner, Robert Morris, Jn., owned the old Columbia Foundry in Washington, which supplied guns and ammunition for the war of 1812.

This building survived the burning of the city by the British in 1814. Mr Foxall was so grateful to Lord, to whom he gave the credit for saving it, that he built the church still known as Foundry Methodist. It now stands at 1500 16th Street.

PRAYERS

FOR OUR COUNTRY.

For thou, Lord wilt bless the righteous;
with favor wilt thou compass him as with a shield.
Psalm 5. 12.

Our defense is of God which saveth the upright
in heart. Psalm 7.10.

America is great because it is good,
but if America ceases to be good,
it will cease to be great.

Alexis de Tocqueville.

We stand before Thee, oh God, on this day and in the capital city of this nation, only a few days after our celebration of the festival of Christmas and only a few weeks before the beginning of the period that we call Lent, between the two seasons in Christian reckoning that are the Alpha and the Omega. But also in between now, we stand at the threshold of a new governmental and national year.

May it be that our recollections and our convictions about the Spirit of Chirstmas will not evaporate, but will linger and permeate our dealings and responsibilities one with another. And as we embark upon our duties and our deliberations of the year we are mindful of the words of Moses to Israel:

"For this law I enjoin on you today is not beyond your strength. The word is very near to you. It is in your heart for your observance. See, today I set before you life and prosperity, or death and disaster. If you obey the commandments of your God that I enjoin on you today, if you love your God and follow His ways, if you keep His commandments, His laws, His customs, your God will bless you. But if your heart strays, if you refuse to listen, if you let yourself be drawn into worshipping other gods and serving them, I tell you today you will most certainly perish. So I set before you life or death; the blessing or the curse. Choose life so that you and your descendants may live."

Help us to remember those words.

And may we also be mindful of the mandate from the apostle:

"Let love be genuine and hate what is evil and hold fast to what is good. Rejoice in your hope. Be patient in tribulation. Be constant in prayer. Rejoice with those who rejoice. Weep with those who weep. Live in harmony with one another. Repay no one evil with evil, but take thought for what is noble in the sight of all. If possible, so far as it depends upon you, live peaceably with all."

Help us to remember those words. And finally, may we so far as our country is concerned, be mindful of the words of one who in this city some thirty years ago, prayed fervently and earnestly in this fashion:

22

"Our Father, we pray for this land. We need thy help in this time. May we begin to see that all true Americanism begins in being faithful to Thee, that it can have no other foundation, as it has no other roots. To Thy glory was this republic established, for the advantage of the Christian faith did the founding fathers give their life's heritage passed down to us. We would pray that all over this land there may be a return to the faith of those men and women who trusted in God as they faced the perils and the dangers of the frontier, raising a standard of faith to which men have been willing to repair down through the years. Thou didst bless their efforts. Thou didst bless America. Thou hast made her great. Would Thou also make her good. Guide us in all this, so that as the year goes on and the days pass, we may know and feel and cry aloud in realization, 'Oh, the depth of the riches and wisdom and knowledge of God! How unsearchable are His judgements, and how inscrutable are His ways.' "

The Honorable Harry A. Blackmun, Associate Justice, Supreme Court of the United States. (Congressional Record.)

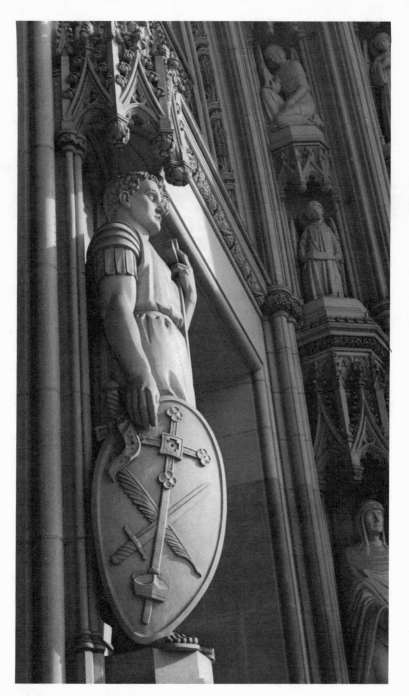

lmighty God, who hast given us this good land for our heritage, we humbly beseech thee that we may always prove ourselves a people mindful of thy favour and glad do thy will.

Bless our land with honourable industry, sound learning and pure manners,

Save us from violence, discord and confusion, from pride and arrogancy and from every evil way.

Defend our liberties, and fashion into one united people the multitude brought hither out of many kindreds and tongues.

Endue with the spirit of wisdom those to whom in thy name we entrust the authority of government, that, through obedience to thy law, we may show forth thy praise among the nations of the earth.

In time of prosperity, fill our hearts with thankfullness, and in the day of trouble, suffer not our trust in thee to fail;

All this we ask through Jesus Christ our Lord, Amen.

From the Book of Common Prayer—Protestant Episcopal Church.

One of the favorite prayers of the Secretary of Defense and Mrs. Caspar Weinberger.

ur Father, God, we thank Thee for the blessings of life in this free land; for the fruits of the soil, the untold resources of the earth, the opportunities for work and play and healthful living; for liberty in speech and written word, for public education, and regard for man's welfare. As we thank Thee for these and all Thy mercies, we beseech Thee to guide us here in all our actions to complete the mission of this Nation to the end that all men may have full civil rights, freedom under law, and a life with dignity and eternal meaning. Make our nation great in that greatness which alone is pleasing to Thee, even the righteousness that is the doing of Thy holy will. Amen.

Written by *Orrin G. Hatch*, United States Senator

We constantly hear about rights and liberties. But, how about duties? Why are there not leagues organized in defense of duties and responsibilities? There is no such thing as a right without a duty.

Rights and duties are correlative, like the two sides of a saucer. It is popularly said for example, today, "Well, I've got to be me. I have to develop my own identity." How do we know our identity? By boundaries, by limits. How do I know the boundaries of the identity of the District of Columbia? By its limits. How do I know my responsibilities, my duties? By limits. By my God, my neighbor, my government, my fellowman. This is how we come to a sense of our duties and our responsibilities. And I wonder if it would not be a good idea to put up a statue on the West Coast. On the East Coast, we have the lady of liberty holding out the torch of rights and liberties. Why not put on the West Coast a statue to duty and responsibility, in which that light is thrust outward to neighbor, in which the hand is open to feed the poor, and in which we will acknowledge as a nation that no one has a right unless he has a duty to God, to country and to neighbor.

Given to the National Prayer Breakfast by The Most Reverend Bishop *Fulton Sheen* (Congressional Record.)

Thou who compassest the whole earth with Thy most merciful favour and willest not that any of Thy children should perish, I would call down Thy blessing today upon all who are striving towards the making of a better world. I pray, O God, especially—

For all who are valiant for truth.
For all who are working for purer and juster laws.
For all who are working for peace between the nations.
For all who are engaged in healing disease.
For all who are engaged in the relief of poverty.
For all who are engaged in the rescue of the fallen.
For all who are working towards the restoration of the broken
     unity of Thy Holy Church.
For all who preach the Gospel.
For all who bear witness to Christ in foreign lands.
For all who suffer for righteousness' sake.

Cast down, O Lord, all the forces of cruelty and wrong. Defeat all selfish and worldly-minded schemes, and prosper all that is conceived among us in the spirit of Christ and carried out to the honor of His blessed name. Amen.

A Diary of Private Prayer, Baillie, 1955
Hon. *Tom Bevill,* Congressman from Alabama.

eavenly Father, we gather together today here in Washington, D.C., the center of government for these great United States. We gather together today, Father, in this place to lift up Jesus, your Son and our Saviour and Lord.

These are perilous times in this world, Father, times of much talk of peace,—but great danger of wars—times of great expressions of hope,—but deep despair by many. Father, as we who serve in these halls of Congress here survey the country and the world, we are struck by the complexity and the magnitude of the problems that face us, as Americans, and the problems that face all the peoples of the world. There are problems that seem to defy solving. Some people believe that man, and man alone, can and will find solutions to all the world's problems. And then there are some people who believe that there are no answers and that we will destroy ourselves, our planet earth, and that time and space will extend on—with only scientific traces to record that we ever existed. But Father, we Christians who gather in your name here today hold neither of these views. We openly acknowledge your sovereignty and power over all of your creation. We believe that you, and you alone, have the answers—that you have a plan. We pray Lord that as we, in the Congress, work on these complex issues facing us that your hand of guidance and wisdom will be upon us. We pray that your will will be done, in Jesus name we pray. Amen.

This prayer was given by *Senator Jepsen* on the west steps of the Capitol before a large group of Christians who were praying for the country and it's leaders. Roger Jepsen is the United States Senator from Iowa. Dee Jepsen is leader of a large prayer group.

EAVENLY FATHER, Though often we do not express it, we thank thee because we have been so richly blessed.

BLESSED-with a land of plenty.

BLESSED- with a heritage of freedom and justice.

BLESSED-with a people creative and purposeful.

We ask thee for guidance in these days when there are those who would wish to diminish our greatness.

CONTINUE to give us the strength for which others wish.

CONTINUE to make our country a hope to which may aspire a champion of righteousness and a defender of humaneness and liberty.

WE PRAY that the women in this room will be guided in their task to be filled with compassion for each other unvexed by fear and with a desire for a world filled with understanding.

IN THY NAME, we ask all this.

Margaret Long Arnold, Honorary President, General Federation of Women's Clubs.

PRAYERS FOR PEACE IN THE WORLD.

Blessed are the peacemakers for
they shall be called the children
of God.
St. Mathew 5. verse 9.

Pray for the peace of Jerusalem!
They shall prosper that love thee.
Peace be within thy walls and
prosperity within they palaces.
For my brethren and companion's sakes
I will now say, Peace be within thee.
Because of the house of the Lord our
God I will seek thy good.

Psalm 122. verses 6, 7, 8, 9.

ord make me an instrument for Thy peace,
Where there is hatred let me sow love;
Where there is injury pardon;
Where there is doubt, faith,
Where there is despair, hope;
And where there is darkness, light;
And where there is sadness, joy.

Divine Master,
grant that I may not so much seek
to be consoled as to console;
To be understood, as to understand;
To be loved, as to love;
For it is in giving that we receive;
It is in pardoning, that we are pardoned;
And it is in dying
that we are born to eternal life.

St. Francis of Assisi.

This is the favorite prayer of many people. Particularly of Senator and Mrs. Russell Long of Louisiana.
The honorable Robert Giaimo,
Mrs. Graves Erskine, widow of the famous General of The Marines and Joan Walsh Cassedy, Oil Industry analyst.

PRAYER FOR PEACE

Mary, Mother of men and peoples, you know all their sufferings and their hopes, you feel in a motherly way all the struggles between good and evil, between light and darkness, that shake the world—accept our cry addressed in the Holy Spirit directly to your heart and embrace with the love of the Mother and Handmaid of the Lord the people who are most awaiting this embrace, and at the same time the people whose trust you also particularly expect. Take under your motherly protection the whole human family which we entrust to you with affectionate joy, O Mother. May the time of peace and freedom, the time of truth, justice and hope approach for everyone... Amen.

Pope John Paul II
December 8, 1981

This prayer is of great comfort to the Apostolic Delegate
H. E. The Most Reverend *Pio Laghi, D.D.*

ear Lord,
Spare us from the insanity of man in destroying
civilisation with nuclear weapons; let reason prevail
so that mankind will never be subjected to another
holocaust.

Leonard Marks
Chairman Foreign Policy Association.

Our dear Heavenly Father, We do thank You for this
morning. Thank You for the opportunity of fellowship one with
another. We thank You that we in this country can be the host
for so many of our friends from over 100 countries around
this world this morning when we lift up our hearts in prayer
for the leadership of this nation and for the leadership of the
world. We ask especially that You bless the President of the
United States, the Vice President and all those in authority
here and in all the nations of the world. And now we are
grateful dear God for the bounty of the earth You have given
us and we ask You to bless it that by its strength we can better
serve You. We ask it in the name of Jesus Christ. Amen.

The Honorable *Harold Hughes,* former United States
Senator.

oly Spirit of God, only source of justice and peace, whose power is love, quicken our senses, stimulate our minds, cleanse our lives, so that our human wills respond to Thy divine will and that, through mercy and forgiveness, the loving relations offered by Thee will be shared increasingly in justice and peace among all races of people on earth.

Help us, we beseech Thee, to pray and to serve for the deliverance of all who suffer hunger, deprivation, injustice and oppression.

Use our talents and resources as individuals and as a nation to enable the healthy growth and fulfillment of every human being, so that each can offer acceptable gifts and services beneficial to wholesome life.

In thanksgiving for the opportunity to offer our best to Thee in the service of others, accept our prayers.

In the name of the Saviour and Prince of Peace. Amen.

This prayer was delivered by the Right Reverend *John M. Allin,* Presiding Bishop of the Protestant Episocpal Church in the United States, to the United States Senate on May 19, 1980. This is the favorite prayer of Congressman *G.V. Montgomery* of Mississippi.

VETERAN'S DAY

hey are again remembered with glory and
thanksgiving.
Theirs is the sigh of pipes, the restless
haunt of bugle,
Theirs is the honour, all the sombre splendour,
Yet all they lived for, suffered, toiled and died for,
                              still is denied them:
                    There is no Peace.

They are again Remembered with laurel and with poppy,
        So have they been throughout the strife-filled years.
        Wars to end wars have come and gone still adding
        Crowds to their hosts who cry with anguished pleading
                    Where is Thy Peace?

They are again remembered and with a new resolve
        Men go their ways to Council and committee,
        Talking of peace, but all the while creating
        Weapons of slaughter, more and more terrible.
                        Groaning they whisper
                    There is no Peace.

They are again remembered, the clangour rises crescending.
        Atombomb, missile and napalm, all nations competing
        Building a Calvary on which the whole universe
        Waits to be sacrificed. O heed Him still bleeding and
                    Grant us Thy Peace.

                                        Serena

    In 1719 John Bradford gave 100 acres, the tract of land called
"Generosity," a Glebe for a Chapel at Ease. This is the site of St. Paul's
Church and Rock Creek Cemetery.
    The Cemetery contains Augustus Sam Gauden's famous statue of
GRIEF. The sculptor called this, the soul face to face with the greatest
of mysteries—If a man die, shall he live again?
    The sculpture is erected over the grave of Mrs Henry Adams.
There is no inscription or date. It stands alone in a grove of evergreens.

THE
VVHOLE
BOOKE OF PSALMES
Faithfully
TRANSLATED into ENGLISH
Metre.

Whereunto is prefixed a difcourfe de-
claring not only the lawfullnes, but alfo
the neceffity of the heavenly Ordinance
of finging Scripture Pfalmes in
the Churches of
God.

Coll. III.

*Let the word of God dwell plenteoufly in
you, in all wifdome, teaching and exhort-
ing one another in Pfalmes, Himnes, and
fpirituall Songs, finging to the Lord with
grace in your hearts.*

Iames V.

*If any be afflicted, let him pray, and if
any be merry let him fing pfalmes.*

Imprinted
1640

lthough freedom of religion and the division of Church and State were considered cornerstones of democracy by the Founding Fathers, prayer was part of all early ceremonies.

George Washington wrote his own Inaugural Prayer and Congress always opened with prayer.

The Chamber of the House of Representatives was used for religious services in the early days of this city by various visiting preachers. The Marine Band played pieces of psalmody to accompany the singers during the services.

It is significant that the first book published in this country was The Bay Psalm Book, a plain volume bound in brown leather printed in 1640. A copy is carefully preserved in the Library of Congress.

The story of how the Book came to be printed is worth telling. The money to buy the press was raised by the Reverend Joseph Glover, Rector of the parish of Sutton, England. Enough money was raised to buy the press, types and paper and Mr. Glover found a young printer willing to undertake the journey and engaged him under contract June 7th 1638.

They set sail for America together with Mrs. Glover and a friend on the ship John O' London but Mr. Glover never saw the press installed, he died on the crossing. Mrs. Glover and Stephen Daye, the young printer, carried on the work and set up the press in Cambridge, Massachusetts.

First to come off the press was the Freeman's Oath, next was an Almanack and then the first book, The Bay Psalm Book.

The psalms were in verse and were considered by the puritan ministers to be closer to the original than the versions of Ainsworth and Hopkins. John Cotton was one of those greatly concerned with the translation and printing of the Psalm Book.

A comparison of the first verse of the 23rd psalm with the King James version is interesting.

The Lord to me a shephered is,
Want therefore shall not I.

Hee in the folds of tender-grasse,
Doth cause me down to lie.

The Bay Psalm Book.

The Lord is my shepherd; I shall not want.
He maketh me to lie down in green pastures.

King James.

The tunes in the Bay Psalm Book are those collected by *Thomas Ravenscroft.*

PRAYERS
FOR VARIOUS OCCASIONS.

The Capitol 1812.

THE FIRST PRAYER IN CONGRESS
December 17th, 1777
By Rev. J. Duche, Chaplain

O Lord, our heavenly Father, High and Mighty, King of Kings and Lord of Lords, who dost from Thy Throne behold all the dwellers on earth and reignest with power supreme and uncontrolled over all kingdoms, empires and governments; look down in mercy we beseech Thee on these American States, who have fled to Thee from the rod of the oppressor, and thrown themselves on Thy gracious protection desiring henceforth to be dependent only on Thee. To Thee they have appealed for the righteousness of their cause. To Thee do they look up for that countenance and support which Thou alone canst give. Take them therefore, Heavenly Father, under Thy nurturing care. Give them wisdom in counsel and valor in the field. Defeat the malicious designs of our cruel adversaries. Convince them of the unrighteousness of their cause, and if they persist in their sanguinary purpose, O, let the voice of Thine own unerring justice, sounding in their hearts, constrain them to drop their weapons of war from their unnerved hands in the day of battle.

Be Thou present, O God of wisdom, and direct the councils of this honorable Assembly. Enable them to settle things on the best and surest foundation; that the scent of blood may speedily be closed, that order, harmony and peace may be effectually restored, and truth and justice and religion and piety may prevail and flourish among Thy people. Preserve the health of their bodies, and the vigor of their minds; shower down on them and the millions they represent such temporal blessings as Thou seest expedient for them in this world, and crown them with everlasting glory in the world to come. All this we ask in the name of and through the merits of Jesus Christ, Thy Son, our Saviour. Amen.

The first Chaplain of the Senate was Samuel Provost, who gave a prayer in the new Capital in 1800.

 ord God of Abraham, Isaac and Jacob—of Moses and the prophets—Jesus and the Apostles; Lord God of the ages and all peoples of all races, grant that this Nation may fulfill its God-destined role among all nations.

Heighten our gratitude for the blessings so lavishly bestowed upon us; deepen our humility in the recognition of the resources so uncommonly plentiful in our land; broaden our sense of justice to include the deprived and the forgotten of the world; lengthen the outreach of our love and goodness to include all who suffer, the homeless and the hungry, the persecuted and the oppressed.

Sensitize us to the hurt and pain of all peoples at home and abroad. Make us advocates of the voiceless, the weak, the poor, the elderly, the neglected. Let compassion be the hallmark of our deliberations.

We pray this is in the matchless name of Him who in love gave His life for all peoples. Amen.

Convening prayer given by *The Reverend Doctor Richard Halverson,* Chaplain of the United States Senate, Feb. 6th 1981.

ive unto us, O Lord, the spirit of
brightness and of courage.
Let not any shadow oppress our spirits
lest our gloom should darken
the light by which others have to live.
Help us to play the man and so to
help others to face courageously
whatsoever tomorrow may bring them
for the sake of Jesus Christ our Lord. Amen.

The Honorable Elizabeth Hanford Dole, assistant
to the President for Public Liaison, is married to
Senator Robert Dole of Kansas. Elizabeth finds this prayer
of great inspiration and uses it regularly although
it was not written by her.

ur, Father, which art in Heaven Hallowed be Thy Name.

Thy kingdom come, They will be done In earth, as it is in Heaven.

Give us this day our daily bread.

And forgive us our trespasses As we forgive those that trespass against us.

And deliver us from evil For Thine is the Kingdom The power and the glory Forever. Amen.

The Lord's prayer is the favorite of *Howard H. Baker, Jr.* United States Senator, from Tennessee.

ive us, O God, the vision which can see Thy love in the world in spite of human failure. Give us the faith to trust the goodness in spite of our ignorance and weakness.

Give us the knowledge that we may continue to pray with understanding hearts, and show us what each one of us can do to set forward the coming of the day of universal peace. Amen.

Frank Borman, commander of the Apollo 8 spaceship, offered this prayer from lunar orbit on Christmas Eve. Frank Borman is a lay reader and takes part in services in churches near his home.

eavenly Father, We give thanks for the simplicity of the Gospel. And yet we realize that these great simplicities, transferred into the light of our time, have the power to remake the world.

If we have lost our sense of unity, one with the other; if we have fled from ourselves, and hence from Thee, help us to find the way. In that way, we may do our part in changing the world.

Today, we bow in humility when we remember the Love that went to the Cross and acknowledge our unworthiness at so great a sacrifice.

Help us today. Help us to join in unity and reconciliation. Help us all to be worthy.

Help us in our time to keep our faith in Thee and in each other. Amen.

The Honorable Walter Washington, former Mayor of Washington, D.C.

rust in the Lord with all thine heart; and lean not unto thine own understanding. In all thy ways acknowledge Him and he shall direct thy paths. Proverbs, 3. 5-6.

One of the favorite pieces of Scripture of *Charles Percy,* United States Senator, Illinois.

Lord God of our Father Israel, praise your name for ever and ever! Yours is the mighty power and glory and victory and majesty. Everything in the heavens and earth is yours, O Lord, and this is your kingdom. We adore you as living in control of everything. Riches and honor come from you alone, and you are Ruler of all mankind; your hand controls power and might, and it is at your discretion that men are made great and given strength. Our God, we thank you and praise your glorious name.

The Living Bible. Roman 1 Chronicles, 29. 10-.3.

This is the favorite prayer of *Arthur Burns,* United States Ambassador to West Germany, formerly chairman of the Federal Reserve Board. Arthur Burns says the evening prayers for his family regularly. Helen Burns is Vice President of the Academy of Poetry and is responsible for encouraging many young poets.

elp us, Father, to be free from our agendas, our schedules, our ministries, our clubs, our institutions, and read and hear and believe and trust in your Word.

We claim that for this morning. We claim that for this day. We claim that for this nation and this world Lord, and we ask a special blessing this morning for the President and Mrs. Reagan. You have put them where they are and invested in them the authority as the First family of this nation. We pray right now, no matter what our backgrounds, affiliations, republicansim, democratnes, we release ourselves from that right now and we claim them as our family and we pray Father that You would lift them up and that we would each day pray for them.

Lord, when its all over and its said and done each one of us will stand before You, not with the score cards, the balance sheets, titles, labels, none of it. You will wonder Lord, whether we have loved You with all our hearts, all of our minds, all of our souls, all of our strength and you will wonder and you will ask if we have loved our neighbor as our self. Deliver us, Father, from the binds and separations and thankyou Lord, for the opportunity to come together.

We praise Your name and we lift up the name of Jesus Christ today, Lord as one nation under God. In the name of Christ. Amen.

Barbara Williams, Director, Congressional Black Caucus. (Congressional Record.)

> Fear thou not for I am with you,
> Be not dismayed for I am thy God.
> I will strengthen you, I will help you
> Yea, I will uphold you with the right hand
> of my righteousness. Isaiah 41.10.

The Shrine of the Immaculate Conception was completed in 1959, but the crypt was in use in 1927.

St. Patrick's Church which was started in 1794 and completed in 1806, testifies to early Roman Catholic worship in Washington, D.C.

Eternal Father strong to save,
Whose arm does still the restless wave.
Who dost the mighty ocean deep
Its own appointed limits keep.
O, hear us when we cry to Thee
For those in peril on the sea.

O, Trinity of Love and Power
Our brethren shield in danger's hour;
From rock and tempest, fire and foe,
Protect them wheresoe'er they go;
Thus evermore shall rise to Thee
Glad hymns of praise from land and sea.
W. Whiting.

This is the prayer that *Walter Dean Innis,* Rear Admiral, United States Navy, Rtd, and thousands of other sailors, have found of great comfort when at sea. Most mariners say that there are no atheists at sea. A great storm converts unbelievers who suddenly realise that a human being has no control over the immense powers of nature, that only a Supreme Being could bring them safely out of the dangers of the deep.

ur Father, in the depths of winter, we praise the Lord for the certainty of Spring.

As the New Year begins, help us to remember that those closest to us need our kindness too. We thank you because your Holy Spirit helps us to have complete victory over the negative experiences which we sometimes face in our lives.

Grant us the strength and courage to face the challenges and grasp the opportunities of this day.

You have given us talents and abilities.

Show us how you want us to use them.

Give us the long view of our work; and may Thy Will be done; and may Thy program be carried out above party and personality, beyond time and circumstance, for the good and the peace of the world. In Jesus Name we pray. Amen.

This prayer was written by *the Honorable Richardson Preyer* for his men's Bible class. While in the House of Representatives Richardson Preyer was called on to serve on some difficult assignments because of his reputation for integrity and good judgement. He was chairman of the Ethics Committee at the time of the Koreagate scandal. At present, Richardson Preyer is teaching at Duke University.

Washington Cathedral

Although George Washington himself marked the spot on L'Enfant's map where the Cathedral should be placed, its foundation stone was not laid until 1904. Mr Glover, President of Riggs National Bank, gathered together a group of eminent men for the Cathedral Foundation in 1891. Bishop Satterlee was the first Bishop of Washington. The Cathedra, or Bishop's chair, contains stone from Glastonbury Abbey, England, and cuttings from the Glastonbury Thorn were sent by American Express on the S.S. Philadelphia in 1900. The Thorn is growing well.

photographs of sculpture from the Cathedral on pages 24-96-99

by Wendy Gasch.

et us be known as people who are committed to the primacy of spiritual community, and as just and compassionate stewards in service to the needs of all humanity. Let us stand fast therefore in the liberty wherewith Christ has made us free. Amen.

Mark. O Hatfield, United States Senator from Oregon, at the National Prayer Breakfast 1976. (Confressional Record.)

ur Father,
Thy will:
Nothing more;
Nothing less;
Nothing else.

The Honorable Stephen J. Neal,
Member of Congress,
North Carolina.

rust in the Lord, with all your heart, and on your own intelligence rely not. In all your ways be mindful of Him and He will make straight your path. Proverbs, chapter 3.

The Honorable John J. Sirica commends this verse and the whole of Proverbs 3 as a support and strength in our daily life. Judge Sirica was chief Judge of the U.S. District Court and presided at the Watergate trials. (Congressional Record.)

Dear God, I know a few important people
        And I am impressed
            by their position
            and greatness.
But don't let me grow proud
        in this knowledge
            so that I look
            with less respect
        On others that I meet along
            the way:
        the lonely widow down the street,
        the lad who leaves the paper at my door.
May I make them know that they, too,
            are important
        and share with them the bouquets
            life has to offer.
For your love, dear God, goes to great and small
            alike
        in measures determined
        only by our acceptance
            of it.

                    .

written by Marie Smith Schwartz, author and journalist.
Marie is a trustee of several hospitals, health centers and
universities.

ear Father, may this time be a time of thanksgiving for your love and tender mercy towards us, in that while we were yet sinners Christ died for us, and that by the blood of the Lamb we have been redeemed and are joint heirs with Him. May we love each other with tenderness, as Thou hast commanded us to do, and may this nourishing food before us let us run and not grow weary in Thy good service. Teach us to number our days with rejoicing toward that day when we will run no more and will enter that lonely river separating time from eternity, and may ours be the true faith that Christ has risen and will pilot us safely to that distant shore to rest forevermore in the precious arms of Jesus. Amen.

The Honorable Jack Brinkley Congressman from Georgia.

This prayer was given at the National Prayer Breakfast.

ord, Our God, we come to thee in prayer, thanking you for the many, many blessings of life- We praise thee for your bountiful goodness, your gracious provision of a country with freedom of worship and privilege of prayer. We thank thee for our church and church family.

We thank you for our long lives, sixty years of wedded life and our children. Give us the strength to carry on during our remaining years—may you continue to lead us in the paths of righteousness.

Mr. and Mrs. A. M. Schofield; Mart, Texas
(ages 91 and 81 in 1982.)

Mr. and Mrs. Schofield are the parents of *James Schofield,* M.D. former Dean of Baylor College and now Secretary of the Liaison Committee for Medical Education.

rant, O Lord God, we beseech Thee, that we Thy servants may rejoice in continual health of mind and body; and, through the glorious intercession of Blessed Mary ever Virgin, be freed from present sorrow and enjoy eternal gladness,
Through Christ Our Lord, Amen.

From *Symbolic Meditations* by *the Most Reverend Richard Ackerman.*

This is the favorite prayer of *Buffie, Mrs. William Cafritz,* who gives much time to charity work.

Mural St. Matthews Cathedral.

y Lord God, I have no idea where I am going.
I do not see the road ahead of me.
I cannot know for certain where it will end.
Nor do I really know myself, and the fact that I think
I am following your will does not mean that I am
actually doing so. But I believe that the desire to please you
does in fact please you. And I hope I have that desire in all
that I am doing.

I hope that I will never do anything apart from that
desire. And I know that if I do this you will lead me by the
right road though I may know nothing about it.

Therefore, will I trust you always though I may seem to be
lost and in the shadow of death, I will not fear, for you are
ever with me, and you will never leave me to face my perils
alone.

Thomas Merton.

One of the favorite prayers of Congressman and *Mrs.
William Stanton* of Ohio.

ome Lord Jesus, our guest to be,
Bless these gifts bestowed by Thee.
Bless our loved ones everywhere
And keep them in Thy tender care.   Amen.

Emily and *Mary Norris Preyer,* both young lawyers in
Washington, D.C.

ord, grant me the serenity to accept what cannot be changed, the courage to change what should be changed, and the wisdom to know the difference.

The Serenity prayer attributed to R. Niebuhr, is the favorite prayer of the *Honorable Birch Bayh,* Former Senator from Indiana.

h Lord, give me the strength to endure my sorrow and accept it as your test for my confidence and my trust in you.
Give me the wisdom to appreciate the joy and friendship in life as glorification of your power as well as your love for the great and the humble. Please remind me we are all travelers on this earth; that we all should learn to share each day our triumph as well as our disappointment with you for you are our Shepherd. With you sharing my journey, I shall not fear, I shall not be discouraged, until the time you are ready to receive me.

By Anna Chennault, In appreciation of the Lord.

Anna Chennault, widow of the famous Flying Tiger General, is the author of three books, writes several news columns regularly and is active in politics.

ur Father, we come to you this morning praising Your Name, confessing our sins, seeking your blessings and your amazing grace. May we who would be leaders always be aware that we must first be servants. May we who seek to be admired by others remember that when we practice our piety before men in order to be seen by them, we will have no award in heaven. May we who have large egos and great ambitions recall that the Kindgom of Heaven is promised to those who are humble and poor in spirit. May we who depend on publicity as our daily bread recall that when we do a secret kindness, our Father, who knows all secrets, will reward us. May we who compete in the arena of government remember that we are commanded to love our enemies and pray for those who persecute us . . . even those who hold us hostage and threaten us.

May the citizens who we serve as stewards of government be sensitive to the fact that we are human, subject to error, and that while we need their critiques, we also desperately need their prayers. May we never forget that the final judgment of our tenure here on earth will not be decided by a majority vote.

As we reflect on our duty to Thee and our duty to our fellow men, conscious of our sins and transgressions, we praise you, Father, for Your promise that if we forgive men their trespasses, You will also forgive us. As we pray, dear God, remind us of the truth in Thy assurance and the assurance of Jesus: "Ask and it shall be given, seek and ye shall find, knock and the door shall be opened." May we be mindful in prayer that You know exactly what we need, even before we ask, and that we have an opportunity in prayer to listen for Your guidance to us.

Let us each pray silently and earnestly in intercession for the President, the Cabinet, the members of the Executive Branch, the Courts, the Congress, our state and local leaders and the leaders and people of all the nations of the world. Let us pray silently for Your peace, Your strength, and Your wisdom, and let us open our hearts and our minds to Your response.

In Jesus' Name, Amen.   Senator Sam Nunn of Georgia

lmighty God, our Father, we offer our thanks to You for what You are in Yourself and for what You have done for the world. Above all, we thank You for the gift of life, and the opportunity to serve You. You call us not to be served, or lord over others. Our greatness is to be exercised in service. We thank you for this work.

Help us to understand and sympathize with human weakness. Satisfy our hunger for the truth. Strengthen us to struggle against injustice and evil. Father, may your spirit help us to play our part in upholding, in our society, wise government and authority based on consent. Give us the sense to discover and accept the uses and limitations of organized protest. Drive us into politics to help others, particularly those who cannot help themselves, but let it be with patience and real commitment.

We pray for men and women in the task of governing their own lives, for all with unruly tempers or desires, for those whom they harm, and for those who have to decide what is to be done with them. May realism and compassion go hand in hand, never leaving one another in the lurch, and may all who have broken and gone adrift have Your love. Refit them for life's voyage and give them new bearings.

Help us to understand that we can do all these things through Jesus Christ who strengthens us. Father, in all these things it matters greatly who is at the helm. Help us now to put the direction of our lives into Your hands. In the Name of Jesus Christ, Amen.

The Honorable Thomas L. Judge Governor of Montana. National Prayer Breakfast.

ive us grace, O God, to understand what it means to share in the human venture. Help us to call to our remembrance the many generations of those who have gone before, living on the earth as we do, searching for the meaning of life as we search for it, hearing the call of duty as we hear it, entering the struggle between true and false, fighting the battle of right against wrong, deciding between love and hate, even as we do. Join us in spirit to those who fought until they triumphed, raising the level of our common life and broadening the scope of human possibility.

Help us to know that what was done by them, we can do: that greatness of life is not the gift of circumstance but the fruit of high resolve. Let us not say that such living was for others but it cannot be for us. Take away our shelter, our evasions, our excuses. Join us, O Spirit Holy, to the greatness of the venture, until we are ennobled by it and its joy is in our hearts.

This prayer is from The Language of the Heart, by *The Reverend Powell Davis.* Frances Humphrey Howard worked with Dr. Davis for the D.C. Council of Churches and finds this prayer so appropriate in remembering her brother, former Vice President Hubert Humphrey.

ear God, I shall pass through this world but once. Any good, therefore, that I can do, let me not delay it, for I shall not pass this way again. Amen.

Author Unknown.

This is the favorite prayer of Congressman *Claud Pepper* of Florida who has worked so hard to better conditions for the elderly.

ear unto us, O Lord, thy children of the earth!
The joys of thy creation here abound.
The golden sun, the billowing seas,
The zephyrs wafting through the trees,
Proclaim in muted ecstasy
The bounties of thy grace.
While in the still of twilight
Silhouetted 'neath the sky,
The spires of thy temples, in lofty splendor rise
Affirm thy benediction from on high.

Dale Miller, Public Relations consultant for Texas interests.

ot my will but Thine, O Lord, be done in me and
through me. Let me ever be a channel of blessings,
today, now, to those that I contact in every way. Let
my going in, my coming out be in accord with that
thou would have me do, and as the call comes,
"Here am I, send me, use me!" Edgar Cayce.

This is the favorite prayer of *Ruth Montgomery* the author of many best selling psychic books.

We thank thee, O God, for the return of the wondrous spell of this Christmas season that brings its own sweet joy into our jaded and troubled hearts. Forbid it, Lord, that we should celebrate without understanding what we celebrate, or, like our counterparts so long ago, fail to see the star or to hear the song of glorious promise.

As our hearts yield to the spirit of Christmas, may we discover that it is Thy Holy Spirit who comes, not a sentiment, but a power, to remind us of the only way by which there may be peace on the earth and goodwill among men.

May we not spend Christmas, but keep it, that we may be kept in its hope, through Him who emptied Himself in coming to us that we might be filled with peace and joy in returning to God. Amen.

Christmas prayer delived by the Reverend Peter Marshall to the United States Senate, December 19 1947. A favorite prayer of *Senator and Mrs. Jesse Helms* of North Carolina.

efend, O Lord, this thy child with thy heavenly grace, that he may continue thine forever. And daily increase in thy holy wisdom more and more, until he come to thine everlasting kingdom. Amen.

From *Henry Mitchell,* well known columnist and author of several books including THE ESSENTIAL EARTHMAN.

everal weeks ago, I was reading in the third chapter of James; verses 17 and 18 concerning God's wisdom truly spoke to my heart. "But the wisdom that comes from heaven is first of all pure; then peace loving, considerate, submissive, full of mercy and good fruit, impartial and sincere. Peace makers who sow in peace raise a harvest of righteousness." It seemed that the Lord was challenging me to pray these verses for President Reagan in a regular, committed fashion. How applicable and appropriate are these qualities, and I am finding great joy and expectation in making this a regular prayer for our President. I would encourage you to consider this same prayer. It is also my prayer that the President will ask for this wisdom according to James 1:4, 5.

Barbara Priddy, who wrote the above is one of the leaders of Fellowship House. Barbara is responsible for much of the missionary work as well as the day to day administration.

ather, we thank Thee for the blessings we are about to receive through Thy Bounty. Amen.

Author unknown.

O.B. Hardison, D. Lit., Director of the Folger Library, a poet and Shakespearean scholar, promised his wife he would always say grace before meals. He has kept his promise.

ur Gracious Heavenly Father, Our hearts overflow with gratitude for your many blessings.
We are constantly amazed over the loving concern that you show for the smaller details of our lives.

Knowing that you forgive our mistakes and forget them, too, is reassuring for many times we cannot forgive ourselves.

Feeling in tune with you brings contentment and peace of mind that goes deep within us.

Without this we feel miserable, so, please dear Lord, continue to hold us securely in the warm embrace of Your great love.

For all of this, we give you the glory and the praise, In Jesus' Name, Amen.

The prayer was written by *Marian Adair,* who founded the International Neighbors Clubs of Washington, D.C., the Welcome to Washington Club and was closely connected with Alicia Davidson and Dr. Vereide who started Fellowship House. Marian is the wife of E. Ross Adair, former Congressman from Indiana, United States Ambassador to Ethiopia.

Chirst Church – S.E.

The first Anglican clergyman to live in the District of Columbia was George Murdock 1726-1761. In 1795 the Episcopal congregation led by the Reverend Andrew T. McCormick established themselves in an old barn on the land of Mr D. Carroll, one of the original proprietors of the city, moving later to Christ Church, S.E. when that church was finished in 1807.

This Church was attended by most of the Presidents and members of Congress, in the early years. Bishop T. Claggett preached there on Oct. 8 1809. The original silver Communion service given in 1802 remains in the church. John Philip Sousa worshipped there and lived close by. Services in the Old Congressional Cemetery were under the charge of the rector of Christ Church S.E. When St. John's Lafayette Square, was built in 1816, the Presidents started worshipping there. The difficulty of crossing Tiber Creek in bad weather, made it impossible to get to Christ Church.

e do not ask for constant joy,
Nor a life that is free from pain,
But we ask for the strength to accept what comes
And the will to begin again.
We do not ask to always win
Nor always to be the first.
But we ask for the grace to lose with a grin
and never to be the worst.

Attributed to *John Philip Sousa* who worshipped at
Christ Church S.E.

eep watch, dear Lord with those who work, or
watch, or weep this night, and give your angels
charge over those who sleep. Tend the sick, Lord
Christ; give rest to the weary, bless the dying,
soothe the suffering, pity the afflicted, shield the
joyous; and all for your love's sake. Amen.

The Book of Common Prayer (1979 ed.), page 124.
The Rev. Henry L. H. Myers, D. Min. Christ Church—
Washington Parish

Although the first Anglican service took place in Willima Claiborne's Trading Post, Kent Island Maryland, in October 1631, it was not until 1794 that the Diocese of Washington was formed. Up to that time the Anglican churches were part of the Diocese of Maryland which had been placed under the Bishop of London by order of the King in Council, October 1 1633.

After the Revolution a break was made with the Church of England and, because the Order of consecration of Bishops in the Anglican church required an Oath of Allegiance to the Crown, the first American Bishop, Samuel Seabury, was consecrated in Scotland by Bishops of the Episcopal Church there. The Episcopal Church of Scotland did not make an Oath of Allegiance part of the consecration service.

Changes were also made in the Book of Common Prayer such as taking out the prayers for the Royal Family, and for the Parliament. At the same time some changes were made in the hymnal. For instance, the verse from All things Bright and Beautiful,

> The rich man in his castle,
> The poor man at his gate,
> God made them high or lowly
> And ordered their estate.

was completely removed as it was not in keeping with the Declaration of Independence which states that God created all men equal.

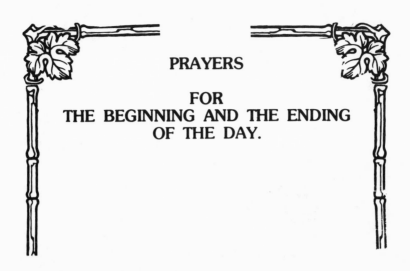

PRAYERS

FOR
THE BEGINNING AND THE ENDING
OF THE DAY.

Holy, Holy, Holy, Lord God Almighty
Early in the morning, our song shall rise to Thee.
Holy, Holy, Holy, Merciful and Mighty,
God in three persons, blessed Trinity.
    Bishop Heber.

O, God thou art my God, early will I seek Thee.
    Psalm 63.1.

I love those that love me, and those that seek me early shall
find me.
    Proverbs 8.17.

Abide with us, for it is towards evening and the day is far
spent.
    St. Luke 24.29.

Each morning when I wake I say,
"I place my hand in God's today"
I know he'll walk close by my side
My every wandering step to guide.
He leads me with the tenderest care
When paths are dark and I despair__
No need for me to understand
If I but hold fast to His hand
My hand in His! No surer way
To walk in safety through each day.
By His great bounty I am fed:
Warmed by His love and comforted.
When at day's end I seek my rest
And realise how much I'm blessed,
My thanks pour out to Him, and then
I place my hand in God's again.

Florence Kellogg author.
favorite prayer of Eliza H. Wilson.

O, God—our hope for the age to come, we see the sun rise on our horizon and we are instantly reminded of *our* dependability on you. We gaze into the face of a newborn child and we marvel at the beautiful miracle of birth. We read of someone who gave His life to save mankind and we are made aware of the power of your love.

O, Lord, give us WISDOM that we might know you, COURAGE that we might act responsibly in Your grace, VISION that we might see the top of Your mountain, and PURPOSE that we might live life in the example of Your son, Jesus Christ, in whose name we pray. Amen.

Nancy, Mrs. Strom Thurmond, wife of the Senator from South Carolina. The Thurmond family say prayers together every day.

lmighty and Eternal God, we have so much to be thankful for. The love that you teach us in Your book. But especially this morning, we thank You for this gathering. We thank You for the fellowship of all of these people assembled and for the love that you have shown. Move that love, O Lord, through these handclasps, electrify it, so that all of us carry it with us wherever and whenever we go. Father, we pray a prayer of thanks to You for the health and strength of our minds and our bodies and our spirits and for the privilege that You give us to serve in Your earthly Kingdom. And now, dear Lord, as we go, go with us, so that each of us, wherever we may go, whichever land it may be, go with Thy blessing, and that we will all be better witnesses and better disciples because You permit us to live, to work and to serve in Your earthly kingdom. And, Lord we thank You for the forgiveness of sins and we thank You for Your Son, Jesus. It is in His name that we pray Amen.

The Honorable Thomas Kleppe

Our Kind, Heavenly Father we bow before Thee this night to thank Thee for our many blessings, for our family and friends and for all the comforts of life we enjoy. We know we have been greatly blessed in every way and thank Thee for watching over us.

Please bless our loved ones wherever they may be—keep them well and safe from harm. Bless us with good health and the strength to do what is required of us.

Bless the poor and needy and comfort those who mourn.

Bless the President of our church that his health may improve and bless and protect the President of our country that he may be wise in his decisions.

Help us to keep Thy commandments and live better each day. We ask this humbly in the name of Thy son Jesus Christ,
Amen.

This prayer was written by *Allie, Mrs. J. Willard Marriott* who uses it every night. The Marriott family are members of the Mormon Church and faithfully abide by its requirement of missionary work, of almsgiving, prayer and service. Mr. and Mrs. Marriott started with one small cafe and built a hotel and restaurant business which is now world-wide.

The Church of Jesus Christ of Latter-day Saints

ow I lay me down to sleep
and pray the Lord His watch to keep.
If I should die before I wake,
I pray the Lord my soul to take.

Polly, Mrs. Jack Logan, loves this little prayer. She always said it as a child and it it still a favorite. Mrs. Logan is a patron of the Arts and is an artist herself.

If I should live for other days
I pray Thee, Lord, to guide my ways. Old Prayer.

Barbara Hackman Franklin was given this same prayer with the additional verse, by her grandmother who had made a needlepoint picture of it. Barbara is a former White House assistant and member of the United States Consumer Products Safety Commission. Now she is a member of the faculty of Wharton School and on the board of several large companies.

Barbara MacGregor, wife of Clarke MacGregor, former White House Assistant, now with United Technologies, has said this prayer for her family ever since she was a child. Barbara simply adds the names of those she loves and asks that they might be blessed.

Keep us, O Lord, while waking and guard us while sleeping.
That by day we may be with Thee and by night may rest in peace. Amen.

Serena.

74

The Chapel of Oak Hill Cemetery, 29 and R Streets North West, was designed by James Renwick. The Charter of the cemetery is dated 1848. Among those buried there are William Wilson Corcoran, John Howard Payne who wrote Home Sweet Home and Secretary of War, E. M. Stanton. The Van Ness Mausoleum modelled by George Hadfield after the Temple of Venus in Rome, is to be found there, also.

Mount Zion is among the earliest churches in Washington. It was a station in the underground railroad during the Civil War. The remarks following parishioners names in the records testify to this. Some are marked, Gone away, Taken away, Sold. This church still has a large black congregation.

THE WHITE HOUSE
Sept 24 1941

Dear Mr Haynes,
   I am very glad through you to extend hearty greetings to all the members of the congregation on the happy occasion of the 125 anniversary of the founding of Mount Zion Methodist. I trust that the congregation will inspire in the hearts of all who participate, a determination to rededicate their lives to the Master.
   Very sincerely yours,
      Franklin D. Roosevelt.

PRAYER BREAKFASTS

 mong the powerful influences in Washington are the various Prayer Breakfasts. Their influence spreads far beyond the city reaching across the nation, across the oceans and skies to every country in the world.

At the National Prayer Breakfast held in the Washington Hilton Hotel in 1981, there were three thousand people in attendance. Among these were representatives from over one hundred countries. At the same time that the National Prayer Breakfast is taking place, many governors are holding Prayer Breakfasts in their own State. Many other people are joining in through the Armed Forces radio network.

The first Prayer Breakfast was held in 1954. It was quite small and was attended by President Eisenhower. Dr. Billy Graham considers it was the influence of President Eisenhower that brought about the National Prayer Breakfasts.

A few days before his inauguration, Dwight Eisenhower asked Dr. Graham to come and see him at the Commodore Hotel in New York and then he told him that he thought part of the reason for his election was to help with the spiritual renewal of America. President Eisenhower asked Dr. Graham for some suitable verses of scripture which he used in his inaugural address together with a prayer which the President wrote himself.

Meanwhile, Dr. Abraham Vereide and Senator Frank Carlson of Kansas, began working on the possibility of a Presidential Prayer Breakfast and enlisted the aid of a small prayer group which already was meeting in the Senate.

Ever since 1954, when the first Presidential Prayer Breakfast was held, every President has taken part. Now, most of the fifty states have a Governor's Prayer Breakfast and many of the major cities hold a Mayor's Prayer Breakfast in the City Hall.

The Prayer Breakfasts are dedicated to praying for those in authority. That they might be reminded that a nation has spiritual as well as material needs. The philosophy is that if the leadership of a country sets an example of firm ethical and moral standards, such standards will trickle down through the whole of society.

Business men's Prayer groups meet to carry out the same ideas in the business world.

Every Thursday the Senate Prayer Group meets and every Wednesday the House of Representatives holds its Prayer Breakfast.

Not all members of the House or Senate attend. Some prefer private prayer, some few don't believe in prayer and some are critical of the prayer groups because they think they undermine freedom of worship and the division between church and state or unduly influence legislation. Some people are against all religiously based groups and are afraid that these groups will force their religious opinions on the public by lobbying and pressuring Congress. However, as members of the Prayer groups point out, they are made up of people from many different religions so they do not represent any one faction. On the contrary, they emphasize the interests that unite humanity rather than dividing it and they do not try to influence politics. A few people doubt the sincerity of members of the Prayer groups and, of course, there are some who are there for reasons of self interest. But these have always existed in every age. In fact there is an old prayer in the Book of Common Prayer especially for them. It asks God to look upon "all those who profess and call themselves christians that they may be led into the way of truth."

Then there is also the more modern safeguard in the saying, "What we constantly think we are, that we tend to become." so perhaps the hypocrites will unwittingly take care of themselves!

That members of the prayer groups are aware of the criticisms, is shown by the words of Congressman Berkley Bedell of Iowa, who said, when addressing the National Prayer Breakfast in 1978,

"There are those in Congress who question this National Prayer Breakfast and their questioning is not without justification. For we read in Mathew that Christ admonished us," and when you pray, you are not to pray as the hypocrites. For they love to stand at the street corners and in the synagogues in order to be seen by men. Truly, I say unto you, they have their reward in full. But when you pray, go into your inner room, and when you have shut the door, pray to your Father."

This mornings's breakfast can only be worth the time if we value it not for the excitement of the crowd, or for the fame of the occasion, but for the opportunity it gives each of us to strengthen our own faith, and to help one another to be a little closer to his God. May this morning be a supplement to, rather than a replacement for our inner room prayers.

My prayer this morning is that each of you will leave with faith, that together we may work to build God's world here on this 20th century spaceship Earth, a world of peace, of love, of caring, of sharing and praying in our inner rooms.

May God bless us all. May He give the strength and guidance to better serve Him and our fellow human beings."

Let your light so shine before men, that they may see your good works and glorify your Father which is in Heaven. St. Matthew 5.16.

God, thou art my God, early will I seek thee. In the morning I will direct my prayer unto thee, and will look up.

O God:

Give me strength to live another day;
Let me not turn coward before its difficulties or
    prove recreant to its duties;
Let me not lose faith in my fellow men;
Keep me sweet and sound of heart, in spite of
    ingratitude, treachery, or meanness;
Preserve me from minding little stings or giving
    them;
Help me to keep my heart clean, and
    to live so honestly and fearlessly that
    no outward failure can dishearten me or take
    away the joy of conscious integrity;
Open wide the eyes of my soul that I may see
    good in all things;
Grant me this day some new vision of thy truth,
Inspire me with the spirit of joy and gladness,
    and make me the cup of strength to suffering
    souls; in the name of the strong Deliverer,
    our only Lord and Savior, Jesus Christ.

Phillips Brooks.

This is the favorite prayer of Elizabeth Pfohl Campbell, Founder of public broadcasting station WETA/26, Washington D.C.

MEDITATION — LISTENING TO GOD.

Come unto Me all ye that labor and are heavy laden and I will give you rest.
St. Matthew 11.28.

O rest in the Lord, wait patiently for Him and he will give thee thy heart's desire.

ethods of meditation are to be found in most early books of prayer. The saints spent much of their time in solitary places, this gave them the time to think quietly of God and to refresh their souls and bodies.

The search for inner peace and the realisation that man cannot live by bread alone, is as old as man himself. Meditation was practised thousands of years ago in China and continued in the East without a break. In the West, meditation became so elaborate that it was looked upon as something for saints and scholars only and people forgot about it until quite recently.

While prayer is speaking to God, meditation is listening to Him. Whenever we lift our hearts in silent prayer we are meditating. It is a way of communing with the Infinite, of quietly contemplating things unseen. Of transcending, or rising above our everyday lives and usual mode of thinking. It means taking an overview or more complete view of earth and heaven and our place in it.

The bible gives many instances of Jesus going apart to meditate, either immediately before or immediately after periods of stress or great importance. For instance, before Jesus chose His twelve apposoles, "He went up into a mountain to pray and continued all night in prayer and when it was day, He called unto Him his disciples and of them chose twelve." St. Luke 6.12.

This night of meditation must have brought enormous renewal of strength of Jesus' soul because we are told in this same chapter that "a great multitude sought to touch Him for there went virtue out of Him and healed them all."

The pace of today requires that we stop and give ourselves a few minutes of peace and quiet at least once every day. In Africa, people only travel a certain number of miles and then they sit and rest, "so that their soul can catch up with their body."

Below are given a few thoughts which some people in power use to bring peace and refreshment to their busy life. These thoughts will help you to relax enough to find your own way of contacting the source of all power and love.

82

o I am glad—not that my loved one has gone,
But that the earth she laughed and lived upon
Was my earth too.
That I had closely known and loved her
And that my love I'd shown.
Tears on her departure?
Nay, a smile
That I had walked with her a little while.

Author unknown.

Sent by a friend to *Barbara, Mrs. George Bush,* in 1953.
Mrs. Bush says; although this is not a prayer, it has been
a great comfort to me.

elp us, O God, to be grateful sometimes for common and familiar things. Let the joy and wonder of them be revived within our spirits, lest we take them for granted, unmindful of them, and our souls grow dull.

For the good earth beneath our feet, for snowy hills in winter, for ploughed fields, for the cleanness of the countryside after rain, for blossoms on the grass, for the shadows cast by great trees: for these, O God, as for the over-arching sky, and stately clouds that pass across it, and the changing seasons and all the aliveness of nature, ministering to us from its strength and awakening our hearts to its beauty, help us to be thankful.

And not less, O God, for all noble lives, bravely lived, for enduring labors and high endeavors, for all that inspires us from the ancient past and has become a part of our inheritance: help us not to forget that from day to day and from moment to moment our own lives are made possible and our experience enriched by those who have gone before us.

Show us, O God, how large a life can grow from gifts like these.

By *the Reverend E. Powell Davis,* former minister of All Soul's Unitarian Church.

In a quiet moment just before he died, Vice President Hubert Humphrey gave this prayer to his sister Frances, and suggested she say it every day as she drives to and from work at the National Institutes of Health. Frances Howard says this prayer helps her never to overlook the beauty of the familiar and to remember how precious are the everyday things when we stop and consider them.

od Bless those friends who make their gardens
With flowers and trees and sweetly singing birds,
With gravelled paths and trees and streams and
    fountains,
Where all the air is filled with gentle words.

God bless those friends who make their gardens
In small backyards where sunlight rarely shines.
Where only loving hands can coax unwilling blossoms
To brighten shadowed lives and darkened minds.

God bless those friends who make their gardens
In tiny pots upon a window sill.
Who gather happiness from every petal
Which even city smoke can never kill.

God bless those friends who make their gardens
Hid deep inside their bravely burning soul,
Where courage waters earth all parched with sorrow
And hope restores what grief and suffering stole.

God bless those friends who make their gardens
Where ever life may take their busy feet.
Who turn the desert into waving cornfields,
And plant their seeds where earth and heaven meet. Amen.

Serena

O come let us sing unto the Lord, let us come before His presence with thanksgiving, and make a joyful noise unto Him with psalms.

For the Lord is a great God and a great King above all Gods. In His hands are all the corners of the earth and the strength of the hills is His also.

The sea is His and He made it: and His hands made the dry land.

O, come let us worship and bow down and kneel before the Lord our maker. For He is our God, and we are the people of His pasture, and the sheep of His hand.

Psalm 95.

Congressman *Richard T. Schulze;* National Prayer Breakfast.

he following are drops of distilled wisdom (or eternal truths) that are spiritually refreshing in time of trouble.

Sweet are the uses of adversity, which like the toad, ugly and venomous, wears yet a precious jewel in his head. Shakespeare.

The clouds pass; the sky remains.

It takes the night to bring out the stars.

Without boulders, the stream could not make music.

From *Deena Speliakos Clark,* Television Star, Producer and Interviewer.

My son asks for his inheritance. I cannot give him perishable treasures that will bring cares and sorrows, but I can give him the inheritance of a holy life, which is a treasure that will not perish.

The Gospel. of Buddha.

am. You are.
But then, I was. You were.
I'm sure of it. I saw it in
My sewing box just now.
Last month I glimpsed of it
Among an accumulation of tools
On the storeroom work bench
When we packed to move again.
Here it is now so plain before me
It makes me cry like a child
This old candybox tin of Grandma's.
She kept it; I keep it
For sewing and mending.
Inside it remnant spools of threads
Used other seasons
On garments long forgotten.
Such an array of shades, colors and strengths.
Scissors, rippers, pics and pins.
Various needles, thimbles, chalk and bobbins.
What common tools and artifacts a family share!
They are the communication threads of spirit
That connect one generation to the next.

Written by *Mary E. Kennedy.*

This is the favorite meditation of Norma Logomarsino,
wife of Congressman Robert Logomarsino of California.
President of the Congressional Club.

ometimes there comes a morn
when all the harmony
of life and love,
and living things
are unified.
When all the brilliance
of mind and heart
and tongue and hand
and nature's light
become as one.

Sometimes there comes a noon
when all the ecstasy
of man and maid
of sky and earth
will blend themselves.
When all the firmaments
of worlds unknown
of seas and shores
and whirling winds,
are softly linked.

Sometimes there comes a night
when all the symphony
of cloud and star
of moon and earth
sing the same song.
When all the eminence
of self and soul
of flesh and bone
of nerve and cell
become Divine.

Then comes the happiness
the glorious laughter
the knowledge sweet
that tells of God.
        Serena.

eiled in Thy glory, O God, canst Thou see us?
There in Thy beauty, O God, canst Thou hear?
The cries of Thy people entreat Thee to free us,
From darkness and guilt, and the hell of our fear.

We have forgotton for what Thou hast made us,
Gone is the light which once showed us Thy throne,
Lost are the garments of Love which arrayed us
When the blood of our Saviour did make us His own.

Tell us again we are made in Thine image,
Teach us Thy Will, Lord, and show us Thy Ways.
Inspire us with charity till we envisage
The truth of Thy kingdom and joy of Thy praise.

Then in Thy pity restore us for ever
Through Jesus our Saviour who bound us to Thee.
For the spread of Thy kingdom, O may we endeavour,
Till Thy glory in man joins in glory with Thee.

Written by *Pauline Innis* during World War II. This prayer
won the first prize awarded by Mowbray, Church Publishers
for "A Prayer for Today."

The Lord shall give thee rest from fear.
Isaiah, 14.3.

Little White Church Under the Hill. 1812.

This first Presbyterians worshipped in homes, in a carpenter's shop, and in the Old Treasury Building until the "Little White Church under the Hill" was built in 1812. In 1946 the National Presbyterian Church was built on Connecticut Avenue and this was replaced by the present building on Nebraska Avenue in 1969.

There have been Presbyterian pastors ministering in this city from J. Brackenridge in 1795 to Louis Evans, D.D. minister of the National Presbyterian Church today.

DOES PRAYER REALLY HAVE
ANY POWER IN THE CAPITAL?

hile many people believe or hope that prayer can influence personal affairs or the spiritual life of the nation, prayer has not been taken seriously as a factor influencing legislation or the policy of this country. Even political and social scientists have overlooked the close connection between religion and politics until very recently.

It was believed that the Constitutional separation of Church had State made prayer and religious belief a private concern and placed material affairs in a totally different sphere from the affairs of the spirit.

Religious lobbies were known to exist, but, as they operated quietly behind the scenes, their influence was not considered important. Now, with the rise of the evangelical and charismatic religious leaders and their increasing use of national television, political scientists and public relations firms are waking up to the fact that they have overlooked something important. Particularly after seeing the influence the Moral Majority had in the last election and in passing some of the recent legislation.

The Black population has long known the value of the power of prayer in gaining political office and influencing legislation. The Black churches have started many a Black leader on his or her way to public Office. As a matter of fact, most black members of Congress have come via their church.

Prayer groups, Bible study groups and churches provide a center for support, for propounding views and for influencing people who in turn will influence others.

Among the strong groups of the general population concerned with future legislation are the various Senior Citizen groups. The elderly form the backbone of the churches and Prayer groups and their number is increasing daily. Like the grass roots of this country and the Bible belt, these people vote for a person they believe has some religious affiliation.

Also, many young people are looking outside the formal religions for spiritual guidance and are following the charismatic religious leaders. These young people all have a vote.

But what of Congress itself? Do our legislators believe in God and prayer? Or do they belong to a church for the sake of appearances and to get votes?

Of course, no one can really know the secrets of another person's heart, but SEARCH INSTITUTE of Minneapolis has just made a study of the relationship of religion and Congress and have reached several interesting conclusions.

One is that in spite of the widely held belief that members of Congress are mainly secular humanists or atheists, members of Congress are just as religious as the general population:

95% of the Congressional sample studied believe in God.

89% are members of a church which compares favorably with 67% of the general population sample.

30% of the Congressional sample had a "born again" experience compared to 34% of the general population sample.

81% of the Congressional sample believe in life after death, general population, 69%.

The SEARCH INSTITUTE study found that there are six types of religious outlook in Congress and these cut across denominational lines. Catholics, Methodists, Baptists, Episcopalians and Presbyterians are spread across all six groups. Evangelical christians are spread across four of the groups. They are not a united conservative force as many people think. One strong minority group of Evangelical christians is liberal voting for civil liberties, international aid and against military spending.

It is how religious belief functions in a person's life that affects voting behavior.

The majority of prayers in this book are not self centered, they are people centered. People whose prayers are people centered tend to be less restrictive in their views and more generous to others than people whose prayer and religious outlook is between themselves and God only.

Then there is the undismissable psychological affect of prayer. This has been and still is, overlooked. Probably because it is impossible to measure it quantitatively. Even so, it exists, as those who have benefitted from it will tell you. As Tennyson wrote in his well known lines,

More things are wrought by prayer
Then this world dreams of. Wherefore, let thy voice
Rise like a fountain for me night and day.
For what are men better than sheep or goats
that nourish a blind life within the brain,
If, knowing God, they lift not hands of prayer
Both for themselves and those who call them friend?
For so the whole round world is every way
Bound by gold chains about the feet of god.

Morte d'Artur.

Prayer can be a great uniting force, since all religions and philosophies practise it one way or another. It can contribute mightily to peace, as it is impossible to kill anyone while kneeling in prayer!

What is this mysterious power which is generated when people pray? Why are some prayers answered and not others? If God knows our requests before we ask, why do we need to pray?

We do not know the answers to all these questions, but we do know that prayer brings results. We know that the human heart needs to lay its burden down from time to time and prayer is one way of doing this. We also know that even if God knows all our needs before we ask, WE do not. When we form our diffused anxieties into specific needs, we clarify our thoughts and, by seeing what our problems are, we begin to see the way to solve them.

Giving positive support to our leaders through prayer can be a great value. President Ford said that knowing that people were praying for him, helped him through the difficult time after Watergate. President Johnson said the same thing when he took office after the assassination of President Kennedy.

A member of the District of Columbia Council who was indicted for misuse of funds said, "It's my mother's fault, she stopped praying for me."

Does any of this prove that prayer has any power in the Capital? It would appear so and, those seeking election or re election for Public Office are considering the best ways of getting the support of the various groups mentioned above.

However, people have become cynical and disillusioned by the revelations of dishonesty, bribery and self seeking among our leaders and are looking for those who reflect the time honored virtues of honesty, responsibility and compassion in their attitudes and actions and who are not afraid to acknowledge them.

The connection between religion and politics is becoming stronger and stronger. The power of prayer is formidable because it encompasses both spiritual and temporal forces. Those seeking temporal power would be wise to remember this and not overlook the power of prayer.

CHILDREN'S PRAYERS.

Suffer the little children to come unto Me, for of such is the Kingdom of Heaven. St. Mathew 19.14.

Your children are not your children. They are the sons and daughters of life's longing for itself. And though they are with you, yet they belong not to you. You may house their bodies but not their souls for their souls dwell in the house of tomorrow which you cannot visit even in your dreams.

Kahlil Gibran.

Many people told us that they still say the same prayer as they did as a child. This suggests that a prayer taught to a child will remain a comfort and stay all through life.

Perhaps the controversy over prayer in schools could be solved by having a minute of silence during which children could say silently a prayer of their own denomination taught them by their parents or spiritual advisor, or chosen by themselves.

od Bless the animals great and small
The plants, the flowers and trees so tall.
God bless the fish and creeping things
And the insects and birds with their soaring wings.

And specially bless old Cissy, our cat
She's cross and spiteful and very fat.
But she's lived with us since I was born
And her fur is getting old and worn.

And bless me too and those I love,
And send some angels from above,
To keep our house all safe and warm
So we may never come to harm.

                       Amen.

Gentle Jesus meek and mild,
Look upon a little child,
Pity my simplicity,
Suffer me to come to Thee.

Fain I would to Thee be brought,
Gracious Lord forbid it not,
In the Kingdom of Thy Grace,
Find a little child a place.

Amen.

Thankyou for the world so sweet,
Thankyou for the food we eat,
Thankyou for the birds that sing,
Thankyou God for everything.

Amen.

For these and all His benefits,
God's Holy Name be praised.

Amen.

For food to eat and health to enjoy it
We thank Thee O, Lord.

Amen.

Old Prayers

e give thanks O God:
For glasses so that I can see,
The things that God has made for me.
For music, symphonies and concerts all,
And I am thankful for baseball.

For friends and teachers, parents, schools,
And boys and girls.
For stars and moon and sun and all,
All these things I'm thankful for.
Heaven and earth and our Savior Jesus,
God I am thankful for Thee!

Written by *Renah Blair Rietzke* when he was ten years old.
Renah, son of Eugene and Lily Lou Rietzke, founded The
World Youth Peace Movement at age sixteen. Renah died
that same year leaving behind memories of a generous,
intelligent, thoughtful young man with a merry disposition and
a true love of God.

For Health and food and love and friends, Father, we
thank Thee. Amen.

Anna Wilson. aged 8 years.

ear God, please bless a little child
And help me to be good and kind
To all the people who love me
And all I love, especially
        My Dad and Mommy, sister, too,
Grandpa and grandma and the two
Uncles and aunts and all my relations
And all the children of other nations.

I know I am also supposed to pray
For those I don't like, but I'll only say
A tiny prayer for them and so
Just bless them a little before you go.

I thankyou for my happy days
And nights of peaceful sleep and rest.
For health and strength and many ways
Of learning things like where birds nest.

I thankyou for the food I eat
And for my toys and clothes and things.
And for my school and swimming meet
and Jungle gym and ball and swings.
Thankyou for everything dear Lord
And bless you too, because you're good.

                              Amen.

entle Jesus
Hold me tight
Cradle me
Throughout the night.
Make me well
So I can try
To catch a
Pretty butterfly.

To tend to all
My dollies needs
To plant my
Little flower seeds.
There's Mother's
Icing bowl to lick,
I'm much too
Busy to be sick.

And God I know
You're everywhere.
I know you're
Listening to my prayer.
Bless my Daddy
And my Mother
Don't forget
My little brother.
Grandma, Grandpa
That will do
Except, dear God,
Please bless me too.

This prayer was written by Congressman and *Mrs.*
Clarence Brown to comfort a sick child.
Congressman Brown has just announced his candidacy
for the Governorship of his State of Ohio.

The loss of a child is one of the hardest things the human heart can bear or understand. Some parents, when they learn their child has a terminal illness, are unable to pray. Others find comfort by laying their sorrow at the feet of God.

Below are some prayers which have sustained parents of sick and dying children.

 Lord, bless and protect this our beloved child. Grant that his/her sufferings may be eased and strength given to his body and soul. Give us the strength to help and comfort him.

Support us through this time of trial and, in thy mercy bring healing to us all. Amen.   Anonymous.

, God, heal this child so that she may laugh and play again with her little friends and learn the joys of this world as well as its sorrows. Heal her so that she may grow in grace and wisdom as her body grows in health and strength. We ask this in the name of your beloved son Jesus Christ. Amen.   Anonymous.

 Thou, who was once a little child, keep this our child from harm. Look with pity on his sufferings and ease all his pain.

Help us to help our child through this illness, so that we may live together to praise Thee. Amen.
Anonymous

God,
Although I do not know why my child should be
taken from me, yet I will try to understand.
Although I cannot pray as once I prayed because
my heart is too raw and bleeding, yet I will not
forget that God is there.

Although I cannot say, Thy will be done, yet I will try
to do Thy will.

Although I am too full of grief to ease the pain of others,
yet I will remember that others also have their pain.

Although my frozen heart no longer beats with love, yet
I know that God's love never fails his creatures.

I will rest in that love. Amen.

 O God, who lent us this child for a brief
time, Take him gently to his heavenly
home.

Let angels cradle him softly against all
suffering.

Let dreams fill his sleep with happiness and may he wake
to the joy of that place where tears shall be no more. Amen.

 rant us the grace to bear whatever you might send,
O God. If you must take our child from us, help us to
bear the loss. We love our child with a love which is
part of Thy great love and so we know that we will
never be completely lost to each other, yet we would
keep him here with us if it be Thy will. Amen.   Anonymous.

Most touching of all are the prayers of the children themselves.

Lord, I am not very brave. I am frightened all the time. I know you died on the cross and suffered a lot of awful pain, but I don't like to hurt. Please take the pain away and make me strong again and I will be good for ever. Amen.

Katie aged 9.

Lord, I hurt so much that I am not afraid of death. Just to sleep and be left alone without needles and medicine and pills would be enough to make me happy. It seems so long ago that I was out there laughing and playing with the other kids. I know they feel sorry that I'm here but I wish they'd come sometimes. But even if they did, I'd be too tired to talk so its works out O.K. I know I won't be out with them again but, perhaps I'll come back like a ghost and have fun with them and make them laugh with me again. I'd like that if you can fix it up. I'm tired now, so Goodnight God.

Jeremy aged 10.

Picture of St. John's Church

In 1796, William Deakins, a veteran of the Revolutionary War, gave a plot of land for St. John's Church, Georgetown. William Thornton, architect of the Capitol, designed the building and Thomas Jefferson headed the list of subscribers.

In 1821 the parish sank into poverty and the building was used by a sculptor for a few years. Then in 1837, the building was sold for taxes.

A wonderful lady, Helen Steuart, was so horrified that she and her sewing circle friends worked night and day with their needles and raised the amount required.

The holder of the property, William Corcoran, was so touched, that he returned the property, together with the title deeds to the faithful ladies.

Mr. Corcoran became a great benefactor and, after the building was rehabilitated in 1838, the parish went from strength to strength.

f therefore the verses are not always so smooth and elegant as some may desire or expect; let them consider that God's altar needs not our polishings for we have respected rather a plaine translation, than to smooth our verses with the sweetness of paraphrase, and soe have attended Conscience rather than Elegance, fidelity rather than poetry, in translating the words into english language, and David's poetry into english metre; that soe wee may sing in Sion the Lord's songs of prayse according to his own will, until hee take us from hence, and wipe away all our tears and bid us enter into
our masters ioye to sing
eternal
Halleluiahs.   The Bay Psalter.

INDEX

About the Author.

Pauline Innis is the author of eleven books including THE ICE BIRD A Christmas Legend, PROTOCOL, with Maryjane McCaffree and GOLD IN THE BLUE RIDGE. She won the first prize for a PRAYER FOR TODAY which appears on page 90 of this book. She has appeared on many national and local TV and radio shows.

Pauline Innis is on the Board of Trustees of the Medical College of Pennsylvania and is the Public member of the Liaison Committee for Medical Education. She is also actively involved in Arts and Music.